GHOST FIELDS *of* EAST ANGLIA

GHOST FIELDS
of
EAST ANGLIA

CAPTURING FADING MEMORIES OF THE AERIAL WAR 1942–45

MARTIN W. BOWMAN

HALSGROVE

First published in Great Britain in 2007
Reprinted in 2011

British Library Cataloguing-in-Publication Data
A CIP record for this title is available from the British Library

ISBN 978 1 84114 653 9

HALSGROVE
Halsgrove House,
Ryelands Business Park,
Bagley Road, Wellington, Somerset TA21 9PZ
Tel: 01823 653777   Fax: 01823 216796
email: sales@halsgrove.com

Part of the Halsgrove group of companies
Information on all Halsgrove titles is available at: www.halsgrove.com

Printed and bound in China by Everbest Printing Co Ltd

CONTENTS

PROLOGUE

Forrest J. Eherenman, navigator in Lieutenant Corson's crew in the 379th Bomb Group at Kimbolton returned to England in 1966, seeking 'solace, diversion or something'.

'Anyway, it was a soggy day in London when I went to Euston Station and asked about a ticket to Kimbolton. The ticket agent said she had never heard of the place and that in her 13 years on the job she hadn't had to refer to her books to locate any village until that day. She said, "You can't get to Kimbolton from London, you have to take a train to Huntington and start all over or you can get off in Bedford." I was pretty sure that busses ran from Bedford to beyond Kimbolton.

'Unfortunately, I overlooked that it was Sunday, the one day the busses don't run. Except for a Salvation Army band marching down the street, the streets of Bedford were deserted. The pubs were closed except for one that apparently opened its doors to old and trusted customers. They let me in, I suspect, because I looked like an American and it had started to rain. Over a pint of Mild I explained to the barkeeper that I was trying to get to my old air base at Kimbolton. Most of the regulars thought I was some kind of nut, but one little old man said he could borrow his brother-in-law's taxi and take me there and back for £10. After all, he explained not many people besides himself could even find the site of the former air base. After some negotiation and a couple of more pints, we settled for £5-10 shillings and we were riding past thatch-covered farmhouses and churches that were only vaguely familiar. It was the first time that I had ever seen them in the daytime. I don't think I recognized the turn off to the base at all. After a ride down what seemed a seldom-used lane, the driver stopped and said, "This is it." "It" was barely recognizable. The macadam runways were piled in fifty heaps of rubble, outlining what had been the perimeter track like those that I had walked "tours" on for various infractions of military regulations.

Inset: 526th Bomb Squadron insignia at Kimbolton on 8 April 1973. (Steve Gotts)

'I located what had been the officer's mess hall, but all that was left was a chimney and a concrete slab. I was surprised to find the concrete slab because everything else that had covered the ground, even the roads to the squadron sites, had been torn up to make way for the plow. The whole place was one big barley field. Gone were the latrines, shops and administrative buildings. All that were left were a few scattered Nissen huts that once housed our crews. I was drawn to one of these, ESP or something and so help me, it was the one in which I spent my sack time in 1943-44. How did I know? It was the stove! No Englishman could afford to fire that monster. We had scrounged sheets of armor plate and conned a friendly Sergeant into welding the pieces together. Six feet, by 3 feet, by 3 feet, with grates at the bottom and a stove-pipe hole in the top. It took a two-ton truck and six guys to install it. Nightly forays to the mess hall's coke bin kept it burning, but we were warm that winter. Though it used to glow red and was a fire hazard, the danger, compared to flying missions, was inconsequential. We noticed that when Colonel Preston made his inspections, that winter, he tarried longer in our hut. He never inquired about the source of fuel, although he did arrange for a 6-foot fence around the mess hall coke bin.

'On the sidewall of that hut, an inch or so above the floor, there is a 45-caliber bullet hole, the only thing remaining in England to show I was once there.

'From a distance, the control tower looked like it always had, but I found that one wall had been torn out to shelter a farm tractor. The steps to the tower still adhered to the remaining walls. I climbed them. I got the strangest *deja vu* sensation when I stood on top, gripping the pipe railing. It was a day like most of the English days I remember, half rain, half fog, and downright yucky. It was not difficult to recall the other times I had climbed these steps and peered into those same skies, waiting to count the number of returning aircraft. The taxi driver took my picture. We got back in the cab and I returned to London.'

The steps to the tower still adhered to the remaining walls. I climbed them. I got the strangest Deja vu sensation when I stood on top, gripping the pipe railing.

INTRODUCTION

American troops or 'GIs' as they were known because of their own derisive term of 'General Issue' began arriving in war-weary Britain in the months immediately after Pearl Harbor. The "Yanks" as they were universally known, made an especial impact. The young Americans with their well-cut uniforms, new accents and money, created a colourful and heroic chapter in the lives of the British people that is still remembered today.

The 8th Air Force and the villagers and townsfolk of East Anglia shared a close attachment that only wartime can create. England 1942-45 was a battlefront. All the civilians were involved in the war effort: as shipyard and factory workers, Red Cross and Land Army, farmers and firemen. Above all they were stubborn, determined fighters who had already endured more than three years of war. Into these lives came the sights and sounds – particularly the jargon – of the men from every state in the Union, as they went on flak leave, R&R, 'liberty runs' and pubbing missions. The impressions they made were profound.

This immortal period of Anglo-American wartime history endures, and the memories never die, for on desolate airfields the rusting and roofless Nissens and Quonsets and dilapidated brick buildings refuse to fade away without a fight. On many a hut wall ghostly images and colourful yet faded pin-ups too are a poignant reminder of the time when East Anglia was 'Little America' to the 'boys in the sky', those who faced the sheer horror of mission-after-mission so long ago.

Martin W. Bowman
Norwich, England

Art at Shipdham inspired by Gillette 'Gil' Elvgren's calendar pin-ups.

1 – The Four Overs

'Americans made love to English girls in many bizarre places and situations. A crewmate made love to his girlfriend in Hyde Park after the "All Clear". Another made love in a shelter. Another in the Underground – in the back of taxis, on the ground under the barrage balloons, in the booths of pubs, in London buses, in trains, in haystacks, in farm fields, in hay wagons, in boats on the Thames, and in the black-out, without knowing who the girl was.'

Staff Sergeant Forrest S. Clark

'By and large the people of England had very good reason to feel that we were "Over paid, over fed, over sexed – and over here."'

22-year old GI Arthur L. Prichard

'I believe the "Four Overs" were justified in many cases. I can understand how an occupying military force, loaded with money, eating the best food, dating their women would draw resentment from an army that had been at war for years, received low pay and only adequate rations.'

26-year old GI William 'Bill' Head

Bovingdon control tower in October 1997.
(Mike Fuenfer)

'Lots of airmen used to ask if I had a sister? "Yes", I would say. "How old?" "Well she's 8 or 9 or 10", depending on what period of the war I was asked. I could not understand at the time why their enthusiasm waned when I told them.'

'Americans came by our house in 'hundreds'. One in Texan cowboy boots shouted to me that he was "The Lone-Star Ranger". At which I ran indoors to tell my parents (I really believed him).'

7-year-old Michael R. Downes

'England to me was a land of Victorian neo-Gothic castles, full of gingerbread and gimcracks, or else authentic battlemented ruins brooding over Welsh valleys or sitting on Cornwall's rocks. England was a landscape laced by railroad lines with stations built like cuckoo clocks bearing names such as "Asses-Milk-cum-Worter". The kingdom was inhabited by amiable bumblers with waistcoated paunches, by droopy knights on droopy horses, by admirals in tricornered hats and by metal-cuirassed dragoons brushing aside great crowds of tight-trousered dandies dripping elegant epigrams. And blooming orange-girls would thrust their bosoms over their corset stays in Hogarthian theaters. My head was full of that literary-historical-mythological view of England, which is absurd but highly accurate if somewhat incomplete, as I later discovered.'

Elmer Bendiner, B-17 navigator

Thorpe Abbotts Control Tower in the snow. (Jim Gintner)

"Building airfields in the desert was easy – in East Anglia it was sure something else... the local population didn't take kindly to us Americans moving in and tearing up their countryside. What with the weather, the cold, the mud – well, fighting the Germans would have been child's play compared to all this. But we didn't blame the people for feeling the way they did. They knew that we were there to ruin their land – and when we had ruined it would then fly hundreds of aeroplanes from this base and low over their homes... there would eventually be 500 buildings of several different types. They would of course be widely dispersed across and around the field. Living quarters and admin buildings were mostly of the Nissen type and there were also the larger Romsey-type huts. The control tower and the parachute stores were built of brick. Apart from the headquarters building, these were the only ones on the site that could be considered permanent structures. The land had been requisitioned by the British Air Ministry and the Government had promised the owners that as soon as the war was over the land would be returned to agricultural use. Hogwash! We knew it would take years to reconstitute the land after the war, if it could ever be rescued properly at all. But that wasn't our problem.'

Bill Ong, an American Army engineer who helped build airfields

'Debach, not far from Ipswich, was a small rural village, encompassing a few individual homes, with the owners devoting most of their time and energy to farming. Since there were no places to shop and no movies, we used Debach primarily as a reference point for other locations.'

Ellis M. Woodward, pilot

Andrews Field (Great Saling), Essex, the first airfield built by US engineers.

Debach airfield.

Operations caravan and the control
tower, now a musem, at Debach.

'We marvelled at the numbers and the cleverness of the
camouflage of the pillboxes. Some were disguised as
farm buildings, with thatched roofs and painted sides.
Some were made to look like brick outbuildings; some
to look like workmen's shacks. Some others had grass
growing on the roof; many looked like haystacks and
water-tanks. They were everywhere. Each main cross-
road had at least one – some had two, thee, or four…'
                                        Robert S. Arbib Jr.

'…Podington in the extreme north-west corner of Bedfordshire…had been built for the RAF but never used to any extent. The field, once a portion of peaceful countryside (the country of Cromwell and Bunyan) had originally been the property, on its western end, of the Orlebar family, whose splendid old mansion, Hinwick House, stood on the road intersection just outside the gate. The eastern end of the airdrome had originally been the property of Lord Luke…'   **John S. Sloan**

'They were building the 'Dromes' as we called them. My father came home one day and said "The Yanks are coming today", so he rigged up a seat on the crossbar of his bicycle and rode me down to a place called Snetterton Heath about 1Ω miles down the road. We waited and in 'they' came – the planes all painted khaki. Within a matter of months we had five different air bases within a radius of five to six miles around the town of Attleborough (where I lived). It was the same all over my region of England, – airfield after airfield – because our region was nearest to Germany.'   **7-year-old Michael R. Downes**

'Can you imagine a gaggle of 18 bike riders charging down those narrow Norfolk roads, in daylight or dark? I can assure you it was not like a Hell's Angels act – it was more like a Wild West scenario where the cowboys came to town after months on the trail and stormed the Longhorn saloon. Nevertheless, these Yanks were totally accepted and – I dare say – appreciated.'   **Myron Keilman, 392nd Bomb Group**

Gunners' briefing room at Knettishall, now demolished. (John Page)

388th Bomb Group and 8th Air Force insignia in the gunners' briefing room at Knettishall. (Steve Gotts)

Knettishall airfield.

'When the Yanks and their aircraft and vehicles arrived, it changed the area beyond recognition. All the country lanes had been widened to make room for the numerous Jeeps, command cars, large trucks and ambulances that proliferated, it seemed, overnight. By this time we had moved two miles down the road to Hopton, to a small cottage right on the road, which meant the road, was slightly wider at that point, an opportune place for two six-wheeled Studebakers or GMCs to pass. On one occasion two of these trucks tried to pass a few yards down the lane and became locked together. I can see now one of the drivers standing on the load in one truck with a crowbar, levering the sides apart, while the other drove slowly along. And the load in the truck? Bombs! They were from the main storage depot near Thetford, heading for the bomb store at Station 136, Knettishall. I would watch the planes take off in the early morning, then when we heard them returning in the late afternoon or evening I would call Mum and we would rush across the fields to the end of the runway and watch them land. Occasionally, there would be a red flare from one of the planes signalling wounded on board. We didn't like to see that. If they landed in daylight they came so low over our house we could read the names on the nose.'

David Calcutt, Coney Weston schoolboy

16

Old Buckenham airfield

'We went back to those airfields in East Anglia from which we flew. We didn't quite know what to expect. Some had said there was not much to see – the fields were now all plowed and sown to barley – chicken coops on old hardstands – runways bulldozed for their stone. But the call to see was strong. We went!… So we came to pay homage – we know that now. Too bad that most of these airfields would soon be completely obliterated. They were hallowed ground to those of us who worked and flew from them… We drove to hanger areas on portions of the tarmac still in good shape… A number of other buildings still stood and like us showed age.

'It was a moving experience to go back again to England. The people of Norwich and East Anglia were as wonderful as we now had remembered them. With old buddies, we fought the war all over again. In old country villages, we found some old friends and made some new ones. But we looked in vain for some who have passed on. All of us hoped they remembered us as fondly as we remembered them.'

England 1979, **Milton R. Stokes, pilot, 453rd Bomb Group.**

Earls Colne airfield, now a leisure complex.

'In no time we kids were chewing gum and eating candy. Real luxury to us because we had been on food rationing for years by then and although we did not starve, food was very basic, to say the least.   **7-year-old Michael R. Downes**

A GI throwing his money around at Mendlesham.

Mess Hall times at Horham. (John Page)

Clown on a wall at Bungay.

'The weather was impossible. Fog and rain. Anything that was not paved turned into brown mud. Crews stayed in their damp, dark huts. They dashed out only to get meals. The humid mess hall smelled of powdered eggs, stale grease and wet wool. Breakfasts were usually green powdered eggs, which came in square boxes, cereal doused with lumpy reconstituted powdered milk, burnt toast and marmalade. Fresh eggs confirmed that a combat mission was in the offing. Some days we had canned grapefruit, two eggs over easy with maybe some bacon, bologna (ugh!), fresh oranges and coffee that tasted of rust.'

8th Air Force crewman.

'Life around the base now was beginning to be a bit move livable and to some degree, like home. The Aero Club Lounge had been decorated by Corporal Ferris C. Parsons, deep sea murals to add a restful atmosphere. Mrs Holman Hunt added the interest in the library and Corporal Gerald E. Brown has painted Robin Hood scenes on the wall... All these things served to make life a bit more interesting and add to the joy of being in Merry Old England.'

452nd Bomb Group History

Cartoons of a GI and a US serviceman etched on the walls of an air raid shelter at Horham.

GI with spanner and rifle at Bovingdon in 1981.

Robin Hood (*left*) and Little John (*right*) on a wall in the former library at Deopham Green.

'I had just turned 12 and was living in Carleton Rode, a Norfolk village sandwiched between Tibenham and Old Buckenham. Our house in Norwich had been damaged in a German air raid. The news that the Yanks in huge four-engined bombers had arrived at Old Buckenham spread like wildfire. Our toy rifles and home-made uniforms, with which we played soldiers, were quickly discarded. We jumped on to our bicycles and peddled furiously up to the airfield. THERE THEY WERE! Some already parked at their dispersal points and others circling the base for landing. We watched in wonder as one came to a halt only a few feet from the hedge by the roadside. The roar ceased as the engines were switched off and the crew emerged, carrying boxes. They threw oranges over the hedge for us to catch. We had almost forgotten that the fruit existed. I shall never forget my mother's expression of surprise on seeing my orange and being told that an American had given it to me. In the ensuing months Old Buckenham airbase was the centre of attraction. Many hours were spent watching the Liberators return from their missions and waiting for a hand wave from the crew as they parked their aircraft. We each had favourite Liberators. Mine were *El Flako* and *Ohio Silver*. When *El Flako* failed to return in November 1944. I was terribly sad as I cycled home.'

Tom Brittan

'When he was eight years old he read Robin Hood the first time. And after that he must have read it 20 more times. Sherwood Forest and Nottingham town, in the days of Richard the Lionheart. He'd dreamed of it then, waiting for the day when he would stand at the rail of a ship watching for England to come out of the sea, out of the haze.'

Bert Stiles

Flying over
snow-covered
Swanton Morley
airfield where the first
American raid was
flown on 4 July 1942.

'I was 'over there' during the most severe winter in a long time. No one in his right mind would ever fly an airplane in some of the weather we flew in. We flew a tremendous amount of flying in about four months, which was a tremendous amount of stress on your body. But we had fun also. We had USO dances. We got passes… The only bad part about going into an English pub, the beer was warm…'

Staff Sergeant Robert 'Bob' L. Schroeder, top turret gunner, 452nd Bomb Group

B-17 mural which once adorned a wall at Podington and is now at the IWM, Duxford. (Steve Gotts)

'...Finally it was our turn. We did not fly to our base; we took the train from Bovingdon to a station near Molesworth and were ignominiously carried there in trucks. When we came to our squadron area, we were not greeted by the familiar, "You'll be sorry," the customary greeting on the State side. The men we saw gave us only a few incurious glances and said nothing to us. Our hearts sank. We were assigned a barracks shared by two or three other crews. Six empty cots gaped at us. These had been occupied by a crew that had not returned from the mission the day before. We were not prepared for this sobering reality.'

Ben Smith

'The Forts aren't named for any particular reason and no one in particular names them. It is a very American process. A pilot from Maine is apt to come out any rainy morning and find that his plane has been named TEXAS. Or the quiet teetotaler who quit divinity school to join the Air Force is apt to come out on the line and find a nude stretching from the plastic nose to the pilot's compartment because his tail gunner (who did not quit divinity school to join the Air Force) knew a guy in Site Six who used to be a commercial artist in St Louis and could still draw a plenty sexy nude.'

NUDES, NAMES AND NUMBERS by Andrew A. Rooney, *Stars and Stripes*, 5 August 1943

'It is 0700. The door to our room squeaks open and S-2 sticks his head through the opening. "C'mon, you're goin' flying fellas; briefing at 0800," he bellows loudly. We wake up – resentfully. Still this isn't so bad. Yesterday it was 0415.'

Captain Howard L. Fogg

'…We did get the week off but most of us went to London. I recall becoming bored within three or four days and returning to the base. Such as it was it was home at the time… One thing that I always found intriguing was the dichotomy of our lives. During the day you could be deep in Germany exposing life and limb and that night be all dressed up and sitting in a theater in town watching a very good stage show. Sitting all around you were people who had spent their day in the office or some other mundane place. I'd look at someone next to me and think that while they were shopping that morning in the corner market, I was standing four miles over Brunswick at 50 below zero with the flak banging around – wild!'

Ronald D. Spencer

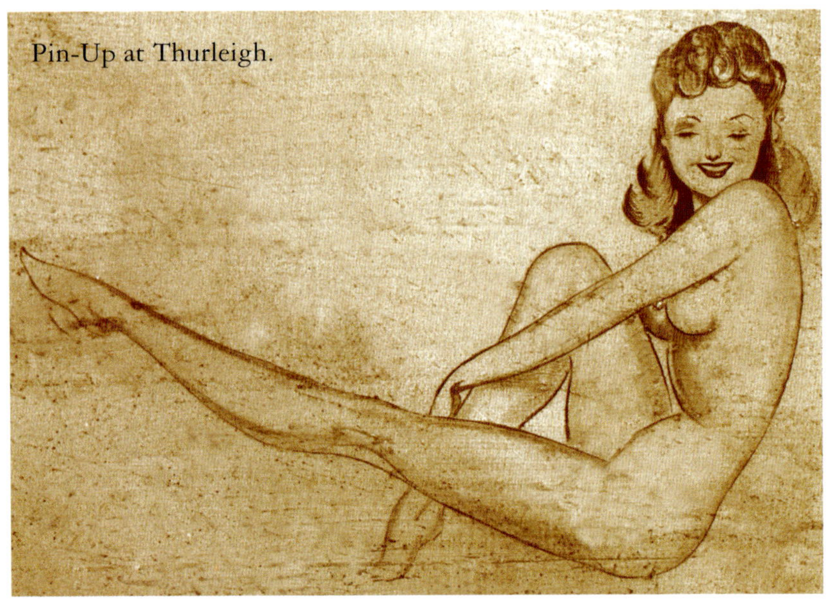

Pin-Up at Thurleigh.

Bottles of wine and spirits on the walls of the old Aero Club at Bungay (Flixton).

'The ground crews lived together so long, we became family', sharing everything, the good, bad and in between. Working long hard hours, we still had lots of fun together. Each cot was put in the same general area in the barracks. The barracks walls were well decorated with pin-up girls such as Betty Grable, Rita Hayworth, Lana Turner, Alexis Smith and Vargas calendar girls…'

**James Tudor, crew chief,
78th FG at Duxford**

'Uncertain of the future, but fearing the worst, we read a prospectus about the 1941 calendar that Esquire is urging on its readers – a dozen pages of nepenthe, each illustrated by Varga, an artist who could make a girl look nude if she were rolled up in a rug. "Order it, look at it, feel it quiver; set it to the music of a slow drum...."'

Talk of the Town, *The New Yorker,*
11 January 1941

'A Varga girl so beautiful, so perfect, so typical of the American girl, that I can put that picture in any part of the world, without any signature.... and they will say: that is the Varga Girl.'

Alberto Vargas, *Esquire* **artist**

'There wasn't a bad body in the bunch. What made them more provocative were their ecstatic poses and their silence – certainly more restful and recuperative than anything offered at the Flak House. I even forgot to remind myself about the war.'

Lt Truman J. 'Smitty' Smith

Snake charmer in the former Aero Club at Bungay (Flixton).

Bar room drunk at Shipdham in 2007.

Buxom beauty on a wall of the hospital block at Kimbolton.
(Bill Espie)

'Each crewman had his favourite pin-ups on the wall behind his bunk. These were highly prized and usually came from '*Yank*' magazine. The favourites were Betty Grable, Chilli Williams in the two-piece polka dot bathing suit, and Rita Hayworth in a silk negligee, the picture that was in '*LIFE*' magazine… I never saw a lewd picture as this was before pornography killed off the pin-up.' **Ben Smith**

'Last night was dull. A dance in the Aero Club proved no different than the others they hold there. Drab looking WAAFs. The music wasn't bad though, played by some GIs… Saturday night Ken Buchner and I went to a dance in Shipdham and what a dance it was. At a dance of similar size in the states there would be at least six pretty girls. This had only one fairly pretty girl…'

Jacob T. Elias, who flew 30 combat missions as a B-24 gunner in the 44th Bomb Group

Names of 487th Bomb Group Liberator aircraft painted in 1944 on a wall at Lavenham pictured in the 1970s. They include – *Sky Master; Spirit of 76; Box Car; Just F/O 20%; Paddlefoot; High Hopes; Our Baby; D'Nif Annie; Lumbering Lizzy* and *The Big Drip.*

'I don't know who started this idea of pin-ups, but they say that it is supposed to help keep up the morale of the servicemen, or something like that… I would much rather wake up in the morning and see a picture of a P-51 or '39 hanging above my bed or over the picture of my wife, whom I think is the best-looking girl in the world, than of some dame who has been kidded into, or highly paid for, posing for these pictures.'

Pfc Joseph H. Saling in a letter to **'Yank'** magazine, 1943

Lumbering Lizzy and *Our Baby (below)* on the walls at Lavenham in May 2006.

(Pete Howard)

'The pilot has just returned to his squadron from two months leave in the ZOI and has been down to the line to watch the bombers return from an early mission. As he pedals back from the ramp toward the mess, he notices the hulk of a bomber lying in the muck as though it might be used for ditching practice. The camouflage paint marks her as an old timer and then his eyes spot the numbers on the vertical stabilizer – 9775 – it rings a bell. He pedals around to the front quarter of the wreck and notes the sitting nude with crossed leg. She stares at him with knowing eyes – so old *Frenesi* has finally bought the farm – the hard way.'

Lieutenant Abel L. Dolim,
B-17 navigator

Squadron insignia at Lavenham in August 1972. (Steve Gotts)

A GI and his girl at Mendlesham in the 1970s (now demolished).

Off we go into the wild blue yonder,
Climbing High, into the sun
Here they come, zooming to meet our thunder,
At 'em boys, give 'er the gun.
Down we dive, spouting flame from under,
Off with one hell of a roar.
We live in fame, or go down in flame,
For, nothing can stop the US Air Corps.
The US Air Force Song

30

*P*in up at Shipdham, one of several at the 14th Combat Wing HQ by Jack Loman using paint bought at Jarrolds department store in Norwich in 1943, photographed in April 1981.

Girl on the wall at Mendlesham in the 1970s (now demolished). (Steve Gotts)

'After chow he wandered down to the flight line. He walked to the next hard-stand where he saw the ground crew working on the engines of another B-24. He smiled at the sight of the well-developed blonde reclining on the nose. He thought that she was a little too raunchy…'

**Robert H. Sherwood,
B-24 air gunner,
389th Bomb Group, Hethel**

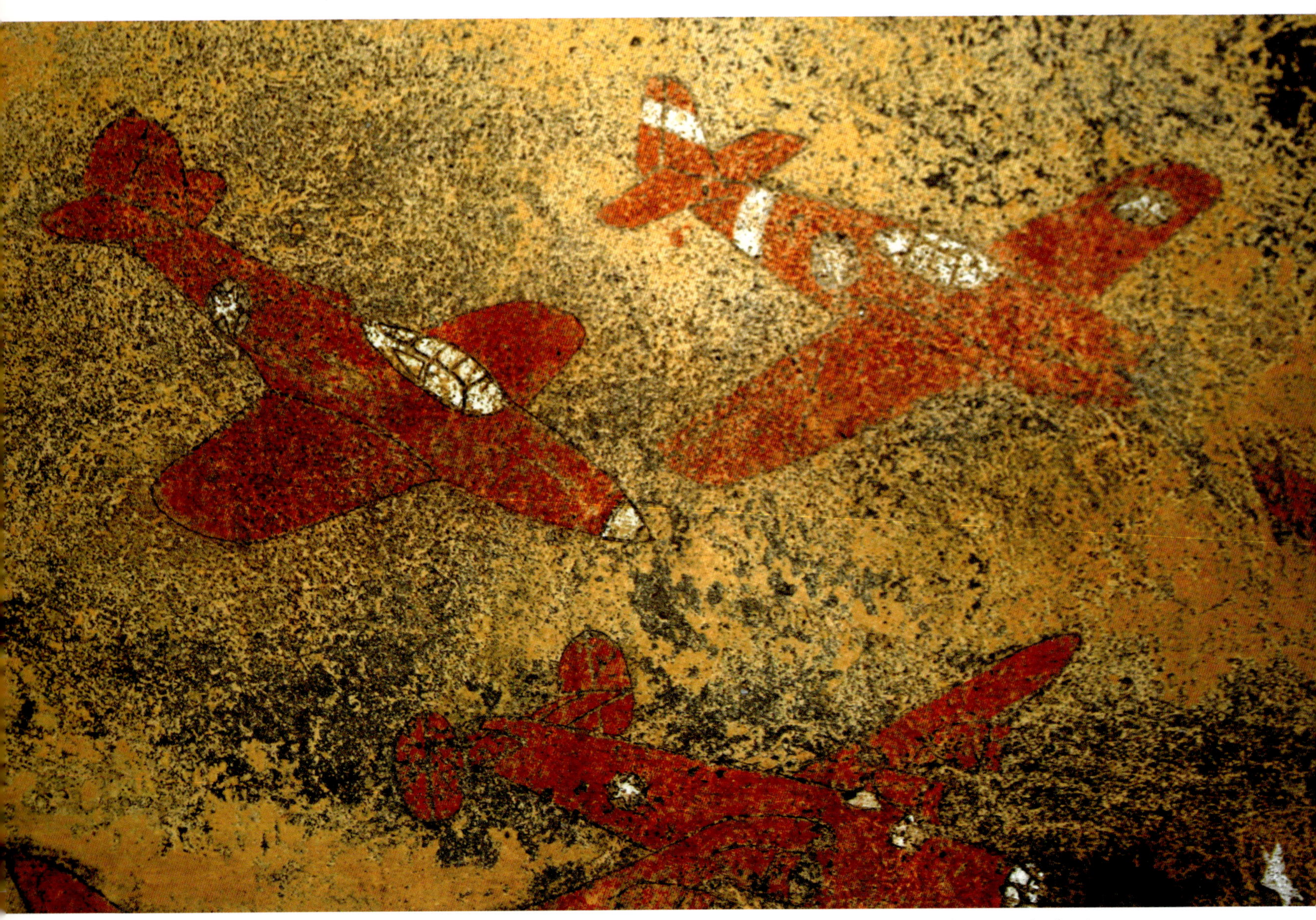

'…I would much rather wake up in the morning and see a picture of a P-51 or '39 hanging above my bed…'

'...The pin-up girls were a pretty lecherous lot. About one in five owned a brassier... Above my sack, climbing, there was a picture of Margaret Sullivan with bangs, a picture of Jane Russell with legs, a picture of a little dream dame called Doris Merrick... and she came out in *Yank*... She had a sort of what-the-hell look on her face, and I used to dream about going back to Hollywood and meeting her in a drugstore on Sunset after she had finished at the studio... I said goodnight to her the last thing every night... Around the top of the room, all the way around were all the Varga girls from a Varga calendar... There were also a good many pictures of girls in various stages of undress and discomfort, drawn by an artist with a mischievous mind, but a modest one...'

Bert Stiles

Nudes that once adorned
the briefing hut at
Raydon, now
stored at
Duxford.

"...Glamour and cheesecake began to gain popularity in the 1930s but during the war America's fascination with the pin-up took off like a rocket. In many cases, the pin-up girl was the soldier's only link back home. Movies were made about pin-up girls and artists. Classically trained illustrators created some of the most memorable, technically exquisite Americana ever produced!'

Jim White, 352nd Fighter Group

"…The pinup Varga Girl in the fox-hole or in the barracks represents all that is beautiful in life, that there is this beauty back there in the world, the world to which he wants to return when the war is over. The Varga Girl represents his girl, his home, his family. This thought is not far-fetched. His girl back home may not be as pretty as the picture of the Varga Girl, but this does not matter. She is a symbol of his girl. If he does not have a girl of his own back home, then he thinks of the Varga Girl as his hope of finding a pretty girl.'
Chaplain James Good Brown.

Her lips, as red as rare Italian wine,
Invite a fire-kiss; her star-hot, white
Pulsating body trembles with delight.
Her legs, encased in hose of rare design,
Stretch coolly the entire length of mine;
And I respond in rather common fashion,
With ardent, fervent, zealous, burning passion;
The moment is ecstatic and divine.

My eager hands will always strive to clutch
Her taunting body garbed in flimsy crepes,
For while the sexy night winds gaily touch
The flaunting squad-room window-curtain drapes
This GI mattress seems to take on such
Bizarre, fantastic and exotic shapes!
Section Eight, Stars & Stripes

Nudes that once adorned the briefing hut at Raydon
and now stored at Duxford.

Nudes that once adorned the briefing hut at Raydon and now stored at Duxford.

'Pubbing missions' were a popular GI pastime. The Mermaid, a short bicycle ride from Seething and Bungay airfields, was known colloquially as 'The Swinging Tits'.

8th Air Force crewman.

Mermaid on a wall of the old Aero Club at Bungay (Flixton).

Pin-ups painted on wooden ammo boxes, which were stripped and used as material to help build a 'line shack' to house ground crew personnel on cold and far flung aircraft hardstands at Hethel. After the war the line shack was re-built as a garden shed and used until it was destroyed in the gales of 1978.

Pin-ups in the control tower at Thorpe Abbotts.

'At Kimbolton we spent the day around our tin-roof hut. Six beds lined each long wall. A chest of drawers stood between each pair of beds. Wooden armchairs – of the sort that pass for garden furniture in second-rate mountain resorts – were placed near the two kerosene stoves that took the edge off the springtime chill. Calendar art glorifying the female crotch decorated the walls and the doors…'

Elmer Bendiner, B-17 navigator

Minstrel and Bass player (right) in the now fully restored Red Feather Club at Horham.

A cheerleader on a wall at Polebrook. (Pete Howard)

Drummer and cellist at Polebrook. (Pete Howard)

Evidence of a Anglo-American tryst at Seething. (Paul Wilson)

'Big' Frank Valesh was given permission to 'slow time a new engine' on his plane *'Hang the Expense'*. His crew consisted of two friends; pilot Russell 'Pinky' Flak and his navigator Andrew Campion. Two American Red Cross girls were also smuggled aboard. With the girls standing behind the pilots' seats, the aircraft started down Runway 28 and was about a third of the way along and nearing take off speed when the tail wheel 'began to vibrate seriously.' The pilot immediately cut the engines and applied the brakes, but the bomber veered to the right and crossed the Field heading towards Farmer Billy Draper's meadow.

Engineering Officer Captain Bill Carleton writes: 'On the way, the right wing hooked the pyramidal tent, which housed our bomb sight repairs unit and much to the surprise of the Sergeant, he was suddenly standing outdoors without having taken one step. The plane continued into the meadow and the right wing struck a large tree and the tree won. However, the airplane continued on and the left wing struck another tree right near the No.1 engine. This tree won also and the unhappy fivesome were now driving an airplane without any wings, but with plenty of gas and a full throttle. They were headed straight towards Draper's barn... By this time, I think all five of them had abandoned the flight deck and were on their way out the back door... Luckily, neither girl suffered serious injury, other than shock and bad bruises and both were able to scramble out of the wreckage assisted by the crew. Campion, who 'was sitting in the nose,' also suffered from cuts. All five were taken to the base hospital but were soon discharged.'

Century Bombers: The Story of the Bloody Hundredth. Two months later at a Court Martial Valesh was fined $100. Legend has it that Valesh 'lost' five B-17s, the first with its characteristic shapely redheaded nude on the nose.

The tree at Thorpe Abbotts that Frank Valesh scraped, 64 years on.

Rose on a shoe worn by the
'Elephant lady' at Flixton.

"...The countryside is quite beautiful with the leaves all turning color. We saw several holly trees with their bright red berries, but on the way home couldn't find the patch we'd seen so didn't bring any home. The leaves are bright green and with the red berries make an unusual picture. We stopped in town and got some apples and a sack of chestnuts, so this afternoon we've been sitting around listening to the radio and roasting the nuts... The insides are white and when roasted are about like the inside of a baked potato...taste like baked sweet potato... I've been chopping wood this afternoon – just to try out my new axe and also to get a little exercise. I think I'll go over and take a shower after I finish this – won't know how to get along when I can take a shower without going two blocks. The Limeys are doing better on the hot water lately, and we've been having hot water to shave with. Believe it or not, long woollies are a necessity over here to keep from freezing – don't mind them after I get used to wearing them. It stays dark till 0800 and cold too, getting dark again at 1700. It almost snowed this afternoon... The English are at least 25 years behind in home conveniences, plumbing, and most everything else, and this base isn't even up to that – which isn't out of the ordinary for the army. The stove we have isn't worth a thrup'ney bit for heating purposes...'

Captain Ralph H. Elliott

'We more or less slept and kept to our own base.'
S/Sgt Robert 'Bob' L. Schroeder, top turret gunner, 452nd Bomb Group, Deopham Green

Circus performer at Flixton.

Theatrical mask on a wall at Flixton.

'…I woke to a flashlight beam in my face, the glare of a bulb overhead and a voice that said, "Briefing at four." I recollect the flow of obscenities that followed with the wistful sentimentality usually reserved for such homey things as the smell of a fire in a hearth or the warmth of a wool blanket on a cold night.'

Elmer Bendiner, B-17 navigator

'One obvious advantage we had in serving in England was the fact that you lived in a highly civilized country with, relatively speaking, all of the amenities. Off the base that is. Outside the gate we had pubs, buses, taxis and within five miles or so a city of some 200,000 people. Thus, we had access to just about everything that wasn't rationed or in short supply.'
Ronald D. Spencer

'The train rides from Thetford to London enabled us to view the quaint beauty of the small towns and rural countryside of England. The deep-green hedgerows, rolling fields and slow-flowing streams of East Anglia were scenes out of 18th Century pastoral paintings.'

James E. O'Connor

Fireplace at Flixton where once a 'Bungay Buckaroo' graced the wall above.

A Day At Cambridge, John D. Preston, *Yank,* the US Army weekly magazine

Signatures and squadron numbers smoked on the ceiling of the Airman's bar in the 'Eagle' in Benet Street, Cambridge.

Hethel airfield.

Young men who flew in bomber-war knew fear as almost friend,
Good clerics' words could often cause their fear of death to end.
And Hethel's chapel priesthood had two who were so blest,
Father Beck and Chaplain Widen; both who stood that test.

Artistic hands with paint and brush made religious decoration;
Their work remains upon the wall "Christ in crucifixion".
They also made a Europe map and beneath some paint concealed,
When later hands removed it. The Madonna was revealed.

Hethel Chapel by Jasper Miles

'It was decided I should paint a crucifix on the wall behind
the altar.'
(Paul Wilson)

'After painting the chapel part of the building a more pleasing shade of light green, it was decided I should paint a crucifix on the wall behind the altar. When I had finished I asked Father Beck if it was OK. He said it was fine except I didn't put the feet together as they should be, but not to worry about it because nobody would notice. Boy, was he wrong about that. However, it was well received even though it gave the chapel a definite Catholic appearance.

Charles 'Bud' Doyle, 389th Bomb Group

'The Chaplain's office became more like a club than anything else. The place was full most of the time with mostly men from the various combat crews that treated it like a second home. I painted the map of Europe on the office wall so we could discuss the various missions as they came up. The combat Mess was just in back of the chapel, so coffee and occasional steaks were to be had courtesy of Tiny the Mess Sergeant.'

Charles 'Bud' Doyle, 389th Bomb Group

Dear Family

I'm sorry I can't tell you… when we first arrived, how we travelled and where we are. However, I can say that England is really beautiful – everything is so neat and orderly. The trains are just like in the movies – only no sleeping accommodations except luxury trains, no dining cars. Sunday we visited Cambridge, which is quaint – no buildings are over 3 storeys. The streets are cobblestone and run in every damned direction! The lower class English rather resent us, however, the middle class and upper bend over backwards being nice to us.

We are at one of the finest Airdromes; the accommodations are excellent. In fact they beat those of my former station. Virginia creeper, ivy and honeysuckle grow on many of the structures and there are lawns, roses and poplars.

The British version of toilet tissue is equivalent to the rotogravure section of the Sears Roebuck catalogue. There are no oranges. We will soon be eating American food tho' I like English food, but they have tried to cook our dishes and have flopped so far. But their hospitality extended that far!

'…In conclusion, I'm well, I'm happy… I like the country, the people and a fraction of the customs.

All my love Sam

Sergeant Sam E. Frisella

50

Corral scene, which once adorned a wall at the 14th Combat Wing site at Shipdham.

'The base cinema was visited by us local kids, where we got in for free. We sat in the front row, or, if the cinema was full, on the floor. If our clothes got dusty we told our parents it was a cowboy film and it was dust kicked up by the horses. I don't think they believed us. Other highlights were the Christmas parties for all the local schools. We were picked up in American trucks and taken to the base where we had film shows, a meal with more food than we had ever seen and a present off the tree from Santa Claus.'
                                                                                David Calcutt, Coney Weston schoolboy

'…We preferred to go to battle with the wry smile of inarticulate cinematic cowboys. In any case, soldiers – whether at Agincourt or Schweinfurt – did not ask why. Throughout our training we had sung the quintessential soldier's song, 'We're here because we're here because we're here because we're here.'

                                                                                Elmer Bendiner, B-17 navigator

'The Americans gave a party for all the schoolchildren in the district between the ages of five and eight. It was held in the Red Cross Club on the base. The children had a wonderful time and I know the boys did too. The boys saved up their candy rations so that every child could have something to take home.'

                                                                **An English girl who lived in one the farms
                                                                on the base at Framlingham (Parham)**

'You asked about coming over after the war is over... 1 don't think I'll ever want to come back. I've seen a lot and of course wartime England isn't at it's best, but there's "no place like home" and I do mean it. So I think your idea of Bermuda sounds O.K… or just a cabin up among the pines and lakes…'

Captain Ralph H. Elliott

52

We saw a truck with a white star on it come down our road, followed by another and then another. We ran outside and began to count them. We were very excited and amazed; they just kept coming and coming, with the dust flying up behind them. From our garden watched the boys get out, while the roadway beside the house became one great mass of khaki, kit bags, helmets, mugs and blankets. The Yanks had arrived!'

An English girl who lived in one the farms on the Base at Framlingham (Parham)

Honington airfield.

'One night a Snowdrop (Military Policeman) and his dog went out on patrol. While checking the aircraft he heard a noise and saw the figure of a highwayman with cocked pistols. He was frightened to death and his dog scooted... There was also this story about a ghostly air gunner who walked between D and E hangars. His head had gone through the gun turret.'

The Horror of Honington

"I had gone to a party in Cambridge and had left late. I was scheduled to fly the next morning and didn't dare miss a combat mission. I got into a taxi and told the driver to take me to Honington. I went to sleep and when the driver woke me and said we had arrived I found we were in *Huntingdon*! He'd misheard my southern accent."

Lieutenant Curtis Smart

54

Looking towards Attlebridge (Weston Longville) airfield from above the A-47 Norwich to Dereham road.

'Stationed at Attlebridge I was frequently on my bicycle whenever we had a stand down. How rich was that part of England, with each village offering history and literature of centuries past! A former student and teacher, I grasped every opportunity to get off base and satisfy curiosity.'

Henry Bamman

Shades of Howard Carter: aircraft paintings on a hut wall at Seething in early 2007.

56

'My Gran did the laundry for two Sergeant gunners from one of the B-24s lost on Christmas Day. Gran had a little cry when the Duty Officer and an MP called to collect the laundry on December 27. One of the gunners would have been 22 the next day and his wife was expecting their second child any day. He had shown Gran photos of her and their little girl. I think he came from Arkansas. He loved the countryside and he often borrowed my old bike. He loved Coltishall down by the river, the Old Horstead water mill and Woodbastwick with its little and very old thatched cottages. He said he would have liked to take one back to the States if he could have.'

15-year old orphan Tommy Dungar

Aircraft paintings like ancient hieroglyphs discovered in a hut at Seething.

October skies near Attlebridge
(Weston Longville) airfield.

'…A map adorned one wall, a map of the United States with the signatures of flyers scrawled over their home states. Beneath the map was a rickety chair and against the other wall an iron cot. At the foot of the cot stood a footlocker with a water bucket on top of it, for shaving. A flight bag and a musette lay beside the footlocker. On a box built to serve as a desk was a coal-oil lamp for emergency use when the electricity failed during bombing raids.'

Skyways to Berlin by Major John M. Redding &
Captain Harold Leyshon. Bobbs Merrill, 1943

A court jester and 'My lady' (opposite) on a wall at the 'Red Feather Club' at Horham.

Horham airfield.

'The most popular man in the squadron is the generous navigator from Oklahoma whose mother sends him southern fried chicken packed in lard in a three pound Crisco can about every ten days. The other lucky stiff is the kid from the Bronx who quite often gets a whole salami from his girlfriend back home. One time the salami arrived badly mildewed and everybody moaned as he chucked it into the trash bucket. One of the guys plucked it out of the bucket, got his trench knife and pared the salami. He sliced it into quarter inch thick pieces, stuck a couple of them on a fork and began to toast them over the pot-bellied stove. No sooner had the aroma wafted around when a mad scramble began for the remaining pieces of sausage.'

Lieutenant Abel L. Dolim, B-17 navigator

Deopham Green airfield.

"Passing the plains and fenlands of that damp dark little country known as East Anglia I saw the towers of Cambridge and Ely Cathedral above the flatness. I could see them from the train window en-route from London to Norwich and back to my base. Frequently I would see these spires partly obscured by mist and a curtain of rain and fog but always when it cleared they stood out firm and inspiring."

Forrest S. Clark

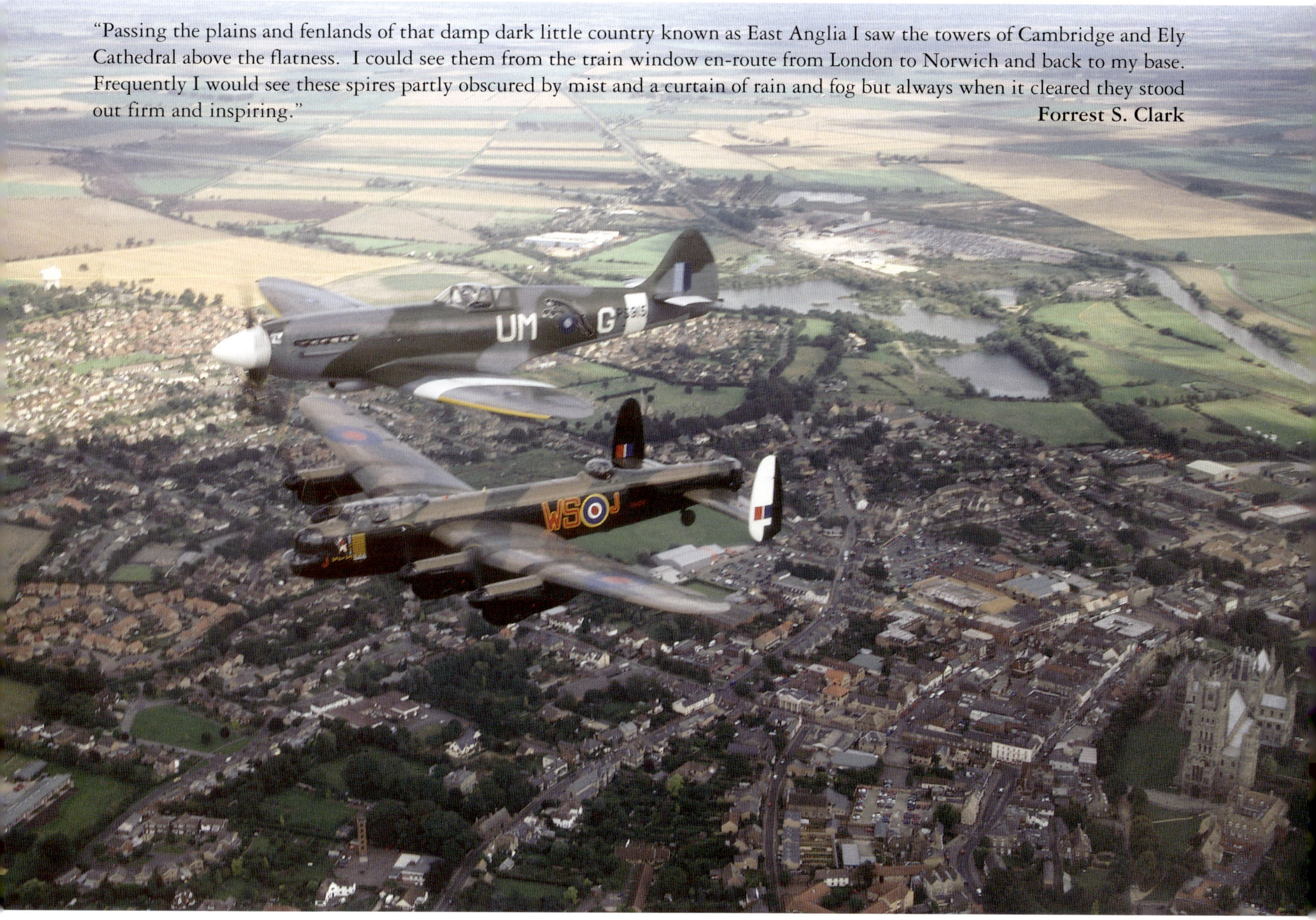

BBMF Lancaster and Spitfire passing Ely Cathedral.

B-17 on the wall of the 'Bronco Bar' at Ditchingham Hall.

Futuristic aircraft on the wall of the 'Bronco Bar' at Ditchingham Hall.

RAF and American airmen's signatures in the Swan Inn at Lavenham, Suffolk. Plaques in the square, church and the Swan Inn, (now a hotel) commemorate the airfield nearby. In the bar there is also a memorial photo of General Brigadier Castle who was KIA on Christmas Eve 1944.

A7 Georra USAAF
Brooklyn, N.Y.
U.S.A
Sgt Clinton W Bruch New York
U.S. 8th A.F.
11 Aug 19
20 Thorne
Rd 4
May 6th 1943
WE KEEP 'EM FLYING
Oscar Smith
112th Cav Recon Sq.
Germany
R.A.F. '45
CPL KURT A KUHL
NEBRASKA
Sgt Leon J. Thon, Jr. Belo, N.Y.

704th Bomb Squadron insignia on a wall at Flixton in May 1991.

4 – Fields of Little America

Unseasonal black August clouds over
Watton airfield and Griston.

'The combat crews were kept separate from the rest of the base personnel and we lived primarily in the NE corner of the Molesworth base in small Nissen huts with 12 men to a hut, making two crews. Most generally, right next door lived eight officers, which formed the rest of the two crews. We had a little coke stove, but toilet facilities were a little lacking. We had a couple of flush toilets but no facilities to take a shower, so we rigged up a couple of barrels with a charcoal stove underneath to get a little warm water. A dirty body at high altitude was so much harder to keep warm and it always surprised me that better washing facilities for the combat crews were never provided.'

Howard E. Hernan, gunner, 303rd Bomb Group

'My hut - where in youth I felt fear, anxiety and a love of life in all that aim of death that held the purpose.'

8th Air Force veteran, 1987.

'It was common to refer to a group by its place name – Molesworth, Grafton Underwood or Kimbolton – when conversing with crews from other groups. They all had euphonious names like Thorpe Abbotts, Chelveston, Steeple Morden or Snetterton Heath. I suppose this is why we liked to say those names. Somehow they added class to a pedigree…'

Ben Smith

'I found my hut down a concrete path that pretended to be a concrete roadway leading somewhere. Huge tufts of grass, knee high to the hedgerow, coarse, triumphant winning grass, sprouting out of spits and cracks, creating natural disorder and chaos of neglect where once we sailed free on cycles so long ago…' **8th Air Force veteran, 1987**

'The hut was in the grip of bramble in the silence of a site where once there was no silence. I knew it as Site 5, now an abandoned wood where a walk can bring the sudden panic of a wood-pigeon, slapping the air, cracking the branches and freezing the spine in plunging fear.'

'As a country boy who spent his youth in Burlington, a small town in North Carolina all of my time in England was one of enlightenment and pleasure. I went to Wattisham and was assigned to the 479th Fighter Group. It was a hell of an exciting time and learning just how war takes place was an eye opener. I appreciated being lucky enough to live in permanent quarters with steam heat, 60ft to the mess and a beautiful lounge. There were Liberty Runs to Ipswich in the black out – hair-raising – to attend movies! The first and subsequent trips to London were out of this world for a little ol' country boy."

Clarence 'Buck' G. Haynes, a Mustang pilot who married his English fiancee, Marge in 1946.

'My hut, sad, decaying, still holding my space and for the young men that have gone forever.'

8th Air Force veteran, 1987

18th Bomb Squadron, 34th Bomb Group insignia (now removed to Horham) at Mendlesham.

Lucky Bastard Club members' names at Deopham Green in the 1970s. (Steve Gotts)

'Got up late for breakfast again today. Bed feels good in the cold barracks. I started two fires but with these stoves you could keep the fires going red hot for 24 hours a day and it wouldn't be warm.'   **Jacob T. Elias**

"On returning from a 72-hour pass in London we saw three planes landing. We joked about that being all that was left of the group. Little did we know how right we were.'

Thomas J. Campana

'We were reasonably comfortable in our quarters. Heat was provided by small pot-bellied iron stoves, which burned coal. These little fellows would turn cherry red when they really got going. We brewed tea and coffee and cooked on them when we could buy eggs from some farmer. The combat crews sort of orbited around them while inside. Even in summer the stoves were needed; there was much chilly weather and it was always cool in the mornings.

'We seldom wore uniforms. Our dress was flight coveralls and leather A-2 jackets. We clomped around a lot in our flight boots, always when we went to the latrine or some short distance, because they were warm. We either went bareheaded or wore the leather fleece-lined gunners' caps. I can recall wearing my flight coveralls for days at the time without taking them off. I would sleep in them too. We cleaned our ODs (wool uniforms) in aviation gas. Consequently, we smelled like gasoline when we were dressed up to go on pass.

'If we wanted to take a shower, we had to go about a quarter of a mile to the showers. There was never any hot water. It was just too much trouble and a very punishing experience; so nobody bothered. Sponge baths had to do. After a time we couldn't smell ourselves; or we thought we smelled all right, because everybody else smelled that way.

Ben Smith

'It was always difficult to climb out of a warm bed in to an ice cold Quonset hut; worse when it was at 3:30am.'
Larry Goldstein, B-17 radio operator

'I had seen her first at a Saturday-night party in the officers' club when she was one of a group of girls shipped up in a GI truck like a load of powdered eggs. They were all proper girls from proper homes. They were to be used for dancing and to be held vertically for light love only. But their laughter tinkled from the barracks in the summer night. Eventually an order came down from Colonel Mo, which read: "All ladies attending Saturday night dances at the Officers' Club MUST be off the base by 0800 Monday morning." Some of the girls, with rumpled hair and heavy-lidded, lustrous, morning eyes, would kiss the boys goodbye before a mission. It was not good for security, but it was pleasant for morale.'

Elmer Bendiner, B-17 navigator

'When we enlisted men reported to the 1st Sergeant, he directed us to go to the flight crew barracks and pick out our bunks. We went and found no empty bunks. On telling the 1st Sergeant of our plight, he told us to go back to the barracks and wait; there will be empty bunks. Shortly after our return to the barracks, supply trucks arrived and all personal effects were removed. How uncomfortable it was to think that our crew made up a Squadron.'

William K. Koch

'Our own hut was untouched by the day's events. The war had come to other huts, where beds were stripped and made ready for replacements with the swift efficiency, which only later we understood to be kind. Thus those who went, went quickly, leaving scarcely a trace. We could then call the war and the Army cruel and feel less guilt ourselves.'

Elmer Bendiner, B-17 navigator

'Operations came in to pick up the clothes and belongings of the other crew. They were last seen on fire and spinning in over Berlin. No chutes were seen. He felt sad. He had not had a chance to get to know them. It disturbed him to see the silent work detail, bundle clothes, pictures of wives and sweethearts, letters, into footlockers. The men were fast but the time went slowly. He hated the gunners who dashed in a little later, guys he did not know. They were looking for stuff to take. Sure, there was a supply problem. They were short of everything, but the attempted raid on the dead men's possessions upset him. It was hard on the men in the hut. They dealt with it in silence.'

Robert H. Sherwood, B-24 air gunner, 389th Bomb Group, Hethel

Crew 51's mission log painted inside a SECO hut at Rackheath by Sergeant Jack Hallman, a combat crew gunner whose bed would have been close by.

'…The shock stunned us all. In the next hut the fellows that we joked with the night before were gone. The next morning there were trucks backed up to many huts, loading personal belongings. My crew learned never to volunteer for missions."

Edmund A. Wanner, 445th Bomb Group

'Deputy CO' sign on a wall at Grafton Underwood. (Pete Howard)

'…After almost ten hours flight time, we found Buncher 12 socked in so we landed at RAF Blyton, 25 miles east of Sheffield. The RAF fed us at their fabulous mess. Women waited on table and there were white tablecloths. After dinner, we went to their officers club for a few lagers and conversation with our hosts. I found their speech accents most interesting. The Canadians spoke like Americans, the New Zealanders like middle class English, the Aussies like Cockneys and the Jamaicans like Oxford dons.

'We stopped to watch some RAF armorers load a 12,000lb torpedo-shaped bomb on a Lancaster, its lower half protruding from a well in the bomb bay section. One of the RAF airmen said to a Yank gunner, "I suppose it will be a long time before you fellows carry one of these (indicating the 12,000 pounder) up in your Fortresses."

'The gunner replied, "It will be a damned sight longer before you guys drop one of those babies on Berlin in broad daylight."

Lieutenant Abel L. Dolim, B-17 navigator

'We had been on a fairly long mission and it was getting late. The navigator looked up the airfield maps and found a RAF base in southern England we could just make. We chose a RAF base because of the NCO pubs on their bases. The RAF crews chose the American bases for the mess hall food.'

Forrest S. Clark

Empty Brylcreem jar at Thorpe Abbotts. (Pete Howard)

Great Ashfield airfield.

'After leaving the replacement Depot the next train dropped us in East Anglia at the Elmswell railroad station, the stop for Great Ashfield, the home for the 385th Bomb Group commanded by Colonel Jumper. The BOQs of the flying officers were some old British barracks with about 8 iron beds on each side of the long building. I scrounged a lamp socket and wired up a bed lamp over mine, using a tin can as a lampshade. We each had a few open shelves to keep our stuff on. My aunt sent me cookies and peanut butter to nibble on, which was quite welcome. I did not keep a diary but I did draw a calendar on the wall by my bed on which I logged each mission, with some details. During the cold, damp nights I slept in my wool long-handles. When awakened for a mission I dressed in my 'flight' officer's uniform. The Germans were extremely rank conscious so we officers always wore our uniform because if captured, officers tended to get better treatment. It was also a sort of superstition to never change what one wore on a mission.'

William W. Varnedoe Jr.

Ablutions Hut at Horham.

'…The average age of the flight crews was about twenty. When a flier had attained 28 or 30 years, he was usually called Pop. We once had a Boston Irish toggelier called 'Pop' Lovett. He was only 32 but seemed ancient to us….'

Ben Smith

'There was a hole in the B-24's nose. The bombsight window was broken, the nose turret cocked out of line. What really aroused his curiosity was the sight of a water truck drawn up in front of the nose. A hose leading from the truck up through the broken window disappeared inside. What were they doing? The ground crew chief was standing to one side of the plane looking lost.

'What's going on?' he enquired.

'The crew chief turned his white and confused face towards him. 'They're washing the bombardier's brains out of the Norden. Flak hit him on the bomb run. Go look in the waist. Go on, look. Come back and tell me what you see.'

'He went to the waist and boosted himself inside. Standing erect he saw the full horror. The walls of the fuselage were hanging with 3- to 4-inch chunks of grey meat. They looked like hacked up chunks of a large fish, bloodless and grey. He took the groundcrew chief away and fixed him up with a coffee in the ground crew's shack before walking back to *Gramper's* hardstand. He wouldn't trade places with the chief for anything.'

'Some of the crews were beginning to fall apart. You could tell when they became quiet, withdrawn and interested in nothing. Some were given to unreasonable outbursts of temper over little things. Some started to drink heavily. Occasionally, a whole crew would just mechanically withdraw. The trick was to hold your mind together. Somehow you had to drag your body along and get the job done. If death came it would probably be quick. Stabbed by a bullet, or a piece of flak. Snuffed out by fire or crushed in a crash. Might just as well forget about it. The best way to fight back was to think that you were already dead.'

Robert H. Sherwood, B-24 air gunner,
389th Bomb Group, Hethel

A corner of England that is forever America at Thurleigh.

Cartoon at Deopham Green in the early 1970s, on a wall long since demolished.

"East Harling, Kenninghall, Banham, New Buckenham, Quidenham, Eccles, North & South Lopham, Garboldisham, Bridgeham, Roudham and Harling Road railway station area were my 'beat'. Keeping the pubs, the dance and the roads, streets and lanes under a watchful eye must have paid off for there were very few problems in that entire area. In December 1945 our military police activity was no longer required so we packed our duffel bags and headed to Honington in Suffolk. No longer an MP. Just a soldier awaiting transportation home and a discharge. I returned to East Harling between Christmas and New Year. I walked down Harling Road to the green, then down White Hart Street, past Tann's Butcher Shop, The White Hart pub, Carter's Bakery, my friends' house, made a right on the lane leading to King Street, then made a right on King Street, past the road to Garboldisham, the village hall where the dances were held, the Bull Inn and back to the green. I had not seen a single soul on that cold, clear and sad night. Everyone was indoors enjoying their first Christmas without war in 7 years. I stood at the green, looked down White Hart Street one last time and probably said, "So long, it sure was nice knowing you."

John Rex, 987th MP company, 2nd Air Division at Roudham near East Harling,
one of the last 12 MPs in the 1192nd MP Company to leave Norfolk in 1945.

'*On the site the cleared patches, the faint outline of a barrack hut in the trees - just a concrete patch, moss-covered, long forgotten. At my hut the shape is there, the number too, flaky white spots on the green stained wall. Bramble and nettle thick around the door, ever open. Windows bursting out in small trees and branches framing the intruders like arboral paintings. Inside like rebellious plants they run amok, tall, heavy, bursting through roofs and windows… The skeleton framework of the roof against the sky leaking in the sunlight in the wrong places and in corners that seemed forever dark.*'

8th Air Force veteran, 1987

Thorpe Abbotts Control Tower Museum.

'Most Post Exchanges (the PX) were drab dispensaries at which lines formed for the weekly ration of candy, cigarettes, toiletries and even chewing tobacco. Not so at Thorpe Abbotts. Before long, ice cream began to emerge from a small PX ice cream factory. Then, in rapid succession, came the ETO's first soda fountain, and, catering to a different taste, the 'Sad Sack Shack,' an on-base pub. Al Paul, who ran the Exchange, opened a first-rate dry cleaning shop, thereby eliminating the hazards of dunking uniforms in 100-octane gasoline, as well as the unpleasant effects of failing to do so.'

Century Bombers: The Story of the Bloody Hundredth.
(ETO was the European Theater of Operations)

Rackheath control tower and summer barley, July 2005.

Later afternoon sun going down at Thorpe Abbotts in December 2006.

'…Because it was closest to the North Sea, Rackheath had more than its share of friendly visitors – and unfriendly ones too. About one night a week we'd receive a RAF plane low on fuel or damaged, returning from a mission over Germany. We accused those 'blokes' of stopping by just to have one of our hearty breakfasts of dehydrated eggs made with dehydrated milk, and flavored with dehydrated bacon bits. What they enjoyed most was to layer on to our 'home-baked' bread, several of the myriad of jams, jellies, peanut butter, marmalade, and apple butter found on each mess hall table. Occasionally, some of our GI blankets, warmer than the RAF issue, departed with them in the morning.'

Colonel James J. Mahoney

'Just before each mission one of our waist gunners had the habit of going off to one side of our dispersal area and when he thought he was far enough so there was no danger of fire he would light a cigarette. The next thing he would do was to pray.'

Forrest S. Clark

…I shared a barracks room with five other officers, one of whom was Tommy Volkman, a navigator from Streator, Illinois. It was a small world. Tommy was the son of the hamburger proprietor at whose shop my family always stopped after a movie during the period between my fifth and tenth years of age and when we lived at Long Point. Tommy was killed very shortly after beginning his tour of duty in late September. Five others of the total of 15 of my roommates in that same room were also killed before seven months had lapsed. Tommy's plane collided with another of our group as it was assembling into formation over a rendezvous point in England. I supposed that his parents were told that he was killed in action and technically he was, but dammit, where was justice in this world and where was there need for this kind of accident?'

Bob Shaver

'Johnson' and *Washington D.C. 'Gee'!*

Bomb log denoting missions flown from Rackheath.

'The Gook' and 'Pauline' Although there was a 467th Bomb Group Liberator at Rackheath called 'The Perils of Pauline' this is a GI and his girl. This and many of the other artworks re-discovered in June 2007 is near the former Communal Site at Rackheath airfield.

"He was 'overjoyed' when the Liberator touched down and rolled to the end of the runway. Hall pulled off quickly to the perimeter track leading back to the hardstands. The rain was an uninterrupted deluge. Christ, with weather like this, you could run into somebody on the perimeter track! They reached the safety of the hardstand. The ground crew were there in ponchos and raincoats to guide them through the turnaround. They looked like drowned rats. How long had they been out there waiting for them to appear through the storm? A wave of affection swept over him. For the moment, these faithful men summed up the idea of home and safety. With five more missions to go was he too tired, too damaged to go on?'

Robert H. Sherwood, B-24 air gunner,
389th Bomb Group, Hethel

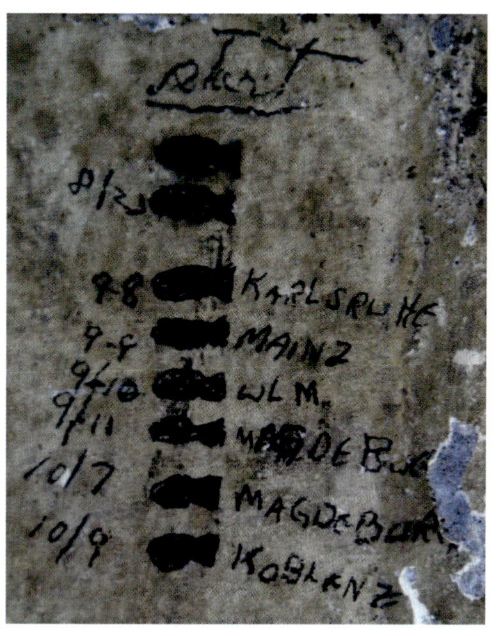

1944 467th Bomb Group airman's mission log. Note *'Split my thumb on this one'* and *Finished!*

Along came JONES at Rackheath.

BOB on a post at Rackheath.

Sack Time, a B-24 Liberator, which was salvaged at Rackheath on 3 June 1944.

'The Bronx gigolo next door has conned the two officers who share a two-man cubicle portion of a Nissen down the line into letting him use their digs while they are in London for the weekend because Maria the Gypsy is coming up from London to spend the weekend with him. Only one or two of the gigolo's close buddies know Maria is a Piccadilly Commando who has such a case on the gigolo she does freebies for him. Sunday morning he bangs into Hut 28 with, "Hey guys, I want you to meet Maria." The Gypsy surveys the troops still in the sack – spots the 19-year-old co-pilot – makes a lunge for his bod and the gang all cheer her effort as the virgin tries to climb the walls of the Nissen.'

Lieutenant Abel L. Dolim, B-17 navigator

94

'Rats troubled us that winter. They ate our dirty socks, shoes, anything. One night when I was awakened by gnawing, I could see a pair of beady eyes glowing in the semi-dark about 6ft away, under the bombardier's bed. Fumbling carefully in my barracks bag, I drew my Colt 45 and calmly blew him to Kingdom Come – the rat, not the bombardier. There was massive consternation and condemnation in the hut until my explanation for firing the gun in the middle of the night satisfied the CO, the sentries and the guys in the huts next door, all of whom came running. The next day all handguns were ordered to be turned in to the armament shop… We impaled what was left of the rat on a metal rod, which we thrust into the ground at the corner of the hut. Until the carcass dried there was a disagreeable odor, but rats or mice never annoyed us again.'

Forrest J. Eherenman

Broken windows at Shipdham.

'One of our favorite pastimes was potting at rabbits with our .45 automatics. There was a veritable epidemic of them in the field behind the barracks. Most of the time we missed, but we killed a number of them. We would carry them to a lady at the Red Cross and she would skin and fry them for us. They were delicious and a welcome variation to our diet. Every combat crewman was issued a .45 automatic pistol. I never figured out why. They were useful for celebrations and shooting out lights. Sometimes that was the only way to terminate a poker game. I once shot them out myself. It got to be sort of a tradition. Nobody got excited about a few rounds being fired off. Almost every morning before the mission somebody would accidentally fire off a machine gun. A round came through the dispersal tent one morning narrowly missing us.'

Ben Smith

'Our air raid shelter was only about 50 yards away, but no one rushed outside to freeze in the cold, enemy or no enemy. Suddenly, all hell let loose as the sound of hostile cannon fire destroyed the absolute quiet. The rookie navigator, sitting on the bed across from me, clad only in his underwear and flying boots, darted out the door. An hour later, he returned from the air raid shelter looking somewhat blue.'

Abe Dolim

Mission log on the corrugated wall of a Nissen hut in 1981.

A hut at Horham open to the sky in 1997. (Mike Fuenfer)

Lavenham airfield. (Mike Fuenfer)

Huts at Deopham Green in 2001.

'When we returned, the left waist gunner, a bombardier from another crew on his last mission, hit the ground, kissing it.'
Lloyd Murff pilot, 491st Bomb Group

'Four men came out of the bomb bay and waist hatch. Then there was a pause. The next man jumped but opened his chute too soon. The blowtorch flame kissed the nylon canopy for an instant and the parachute collapsed. The airman went into a clawing frenzy, his arms and legs thrashing, trying to gain purchase in the thin air. The plane stalled again and spun towards France. No one got out after that.'
Robert H. Sherwood, B-24 air gunner, 389th Bomb Group, Hethel

Horsham St Faith airfield now Norwich Aiport.

'My hut, here in a wood, buried in time like the site, half a century on, fading into nothingness amid the trees in an English countryside.'

8th Air Force veteran, 1987 (Mike Fuenfer)

'The top turret gunner was appalled at the barracks. It was an uninsulated tar paper hut with only one entrance door. This led to a small four-foot-long vestibule with a second door. The wooden structure, one of many huts, was falling apart. Inside were cots for the gunners of five crews - thirty men. There were a few double-decked bunks as extra beds. The hut was full except for six empty cots. The crew quickly claimed their spaces and were widely separated from each other. The top turret gunner was not prepared for the sinister silence, which greeted them. No one yelled the usual, 'I see they've lowered the standards again.' Not a soul announced, 'Here comes the fresh meat!' No one made a sound or looked at them. Looking around the hut an old and torn die-cut sign proclaimed, 'Merry Christmas'. In May?

Robert H. Sherwood, B-24 air gunner, 389th Bomb Group. (Mike Fuenfer)

Thorpe Abbotts Control Tower (Jim Gintner)

Twinwoods control tower, now a museum, near Bedford in August 1994. It is claimed that on 15 December 1944 a Norseman stopped off here to pick up famous band leader Major Glenn Miller to fly him to Paris.

'I thought I could see Red's ghost on the airfield in the early morning mist. "Red" was a mid-western kid with burning bright red hair, so innocent we believed him when he said he had never been with a woman. He grew up on a farm in Iowa far from the cities and from women, except for the girls he saw at a distance. 'Red' was in the crew of a plane off our wing. The time came for the bomb run and the bomb bay doors opened. Then a shout went up over our intercom. "Damn!" The news came back that someone had dropped the bombs through one wing of 'Red's' bomber and it went down. "Poor kid," a crewmate said. "He never had a chance." We were all kids. I was 21 when I started flying missions. In fact, the whole crew was very young, just out of high school or college.'

Forrest S. Clark

Boxted airfield.

Elveden Hall near Thetford, which was
a wartime HQ for the 8th Air Force.

Wormingford airfield.

'The best memory was being collected in army lorries at the school and then being taken to the most wonderful parties at Tibenham given by the Americans. They had hearts of gold to entertain what must have been hundreds of kids. We were shown kindness, which meant a lot during wartime. Sweets were put in every pocket; there were parcels, gifts, film shows and Santa. It was wonderful.'

Beryl M. Sutton

'Came the end of the war and all of a sudden peace descended on our corner of Suffolk, as it did around all the airbases in East Anglia. At the height of the war, it was said you couldn't go more than five miles without coming across an airfield. We settled into peacetime, although we still had rationing — food and clothes mainly.'

David Calcutt

Memorial stained glass window in Elveden church.

'They came and collected us from our homes in ambulances and took us back to the Hospital where we had a great time. We saw a film show and were given toys and sweets galore (in Morley as elsewhere rationing meant that we were only allowed two ounces a week but not here!) There was candy, as the Yanks called it and gum by the yard. The toys were fun – some having been made by the wounded men while they were recuperating.'

Derek Daniels remembering the Christmas Party in the Red Cross clubhouse at the 231st American Army Air Force hospital at Morley, near Wymondham on 23 December 1944.

'The hospital was like a beehive with all the activity! There were murals in the huts painted by the patients.'

Mrs Bernice Pegg (nee Couldham) talking about the American Army Air Force hospital at Morley, near Wymondham

Morley Hospital closed at midnight on 8 June 1945 and went on to become Wymondham College.

Rattlesden airfield.

'One summer evening when everyone else had left the airfield I spent an hour in the hangar at Tibenham trying to free a wheel on a lifting-trolley. Eventually I had to admit defeat. Then I heard a quiet American voice beside me offering assistance and advice and almost immediately afterwards we levered the tyre free. He stayed a while and talked of B-24s and Jimmy Stewart but I neither saw him arrive nor depart and certainly neither heard nor saw a car. I took the crumpled wheel fairing to the workshop and set to work with the hammer. Minutes later I heard someone whistling a tune and obviously approaching along the corridor. Hammer poised, I waited to greet the visitor but the whistling passed the open door – though no one appeared. Puzzled, I looked out along the empty corridor and then into each of the rooms before doing a circuit outside the building. There was nobody so I tried to convince myself that I had imagined it all and went back to the bench. Three times I heard that whistling and three times I searched the building to no avail. Weeks later I was told how one night a Ju 88 followed the Liberators back to their base, shot down three in the circuit and caused two more to collide. I also heard that there was supposed to be a ridiculous tale about the ghost of one of the navigators who was known to haunt the control tower.'

Charles Hall

'You can imagine the impact it had, around 3,000 men arriving in our small village, all with film star accents and many with suntans. I am only glad I was a small child at the time! Our narrow roads were busy with convoys of supplies and there were many young and so-friendly Yanks who stopped to ask the way. They were very good to the children and we were invited to the camp on special occasions for a party.

I can still picture what it was like when the trucks drew up to the school and lifted me over the tail-lift and into the truck. That was Thanksgiving, 1943. There were 85 children and two evacuees in the school at the time.'

Pat Everson, a 10-year old Norfolk schoolgirl at Seething and Mundham County Primary School when the 448th Bomb Group arrived at Seething airfield

Main runway at Seething with the
control tower museum, bottom right.

Sudbury (Acton) airfield.

'They went shouting and singing and waving. We could hear them as they went along the road to the station, until they got farther and farther away, then everywhere became silent. The Yanks had come – and now they were gone!

'I shall always remember that vast contrast when they left. One moment it was all noise, shouting, trucks starting stopping and then dead silence, with everything deserted. I walked back home across the runway. There was no one in sight; it was just as if everyone had fallen asleep. We should never forget the 390th, the boys who had come so far from their homes in America, many of them never to return. For more than two years they lived in and were a part of our countryside and we missed them sincerely when they were gone.'

**An English girl who lived in one the farms on the
base at Station 253, Framlingham (Parham)**

Right: 'We knew we would never forget… the silver fleets of Fortresses droning through the skies like lines from a feather brush; the tower of the Boston Stump like a white sword across the fens; the dank wind from the passing trains flapping the blankets about the thin forms of old women and babies in the underground stations; the blood red of a wheat field brushed with poppies in Hertfordshire and the sulphur of a mustard field in Suffolk; there were the dawn calisthenics in the quiet streets of Watford and the midnight meetings around the fire in the Nissen huts at Debach.

Retrospect by Robert Arbib Jr.

Spitfires over Boston.

"Decided to go take a look around Great Yarmouth. We took a noon train and came back about 8:55pm. The beaches are all closed off now with barbed wire and pillboxes and since the beaches are mined, it's a poor place to go anyway. From Brittania Pier we walked south on the big, wide walk for several blocks. It was quite a resort area in peacetime as the post cards show. There were two enormous dance pavilions, one all glass and several amusement places including a big roller coaster. Then we went to see a show called Rose Marie with Jeanette McDonald and Nelson Eddy. I enjoyed the singing… then we had a real good supper; chicken and ice cream in fact. It got kinda rainy but I didn't mind. That seems to cover the day Vonny.

Captain Ralph H. Elliott

Mirror image at Thorpe Abbotts control tower.

'Luckily, the control tower was left intact and after lying derelict for many years, it was completely renovated by a small band of enthusiasts, as was the site it stands on. It now houses, with several other buildings, the Hundredth Bomb Group Memorial Museum.

'From time to time, an overpowering presence can be felt in the Tower, occasionally accompanied by the brief glimpse of an airman dressed in uniform or in full flying gear. VHF chatter and the sounds of aircraft have also been observed. This strange phenomena could be linked to 'Eddie the Ghost,' who began appearing after the first Berlin raids and who arrived by walking straight through the wall of the airmen's quarters, where he would pace up and down in the dark. This and similar stories persisted for several months. Inevitably some of the men took to their beds armed with carbines and pistols, in the belief that the spectre was looking for its next victim. Fearing an accident, Colonel Jeffrey forbade all talk of Eddie 'on penalty of a court marshal.'

'During the early stages of renovation, the feeling in the Tower was of deep despair, but as the work progressed, so the anguish subsided and the sightings became less frequent. The apparition is occasionally seen when the Tower is locked at night – the figure of a pilot in uniform appears at a first floor window, looking out, as if to say good night. It is not unusual for the person locking up to go back in, thinking he had locked a member of the public inside.'

Century Bombers: The Story of the Bloody
Hundredth

When the night is still...
and the Moon is clear
The ghosts of the past are here
Of men long dead and machines that sped
Into the valley of fear.
The Old Airfield by Peter Markham

'…An old Fire-engine House still stood. Pigs grunted and squealed from a service hut. Here a portion of a red brick bomb shelter, overgrown with rank weeds, caught the eye. These shelters were used but two times in our memory, during enemy bomb alerts. We felt we would rather die in a warm bed than freeze to death in the security of the shelter's frigid walls…'

(Mike Fuenfer)

'…Nearby on closer look the ghosts in the abandoned wood emerge. Lumpy mounds of blast shelters, bearing trees like battle standards, merging into the landscape withdrawing into the comfort of obscurity yet showing their tails. Patches of shiny brickwork beyond the nettles. The abandoned buildings given like gifts to nature, guttered, windowless, rusting deep brown sagging roofs. Thick undergrowth and trees, smothering, engulfing, blurring the outline except the memory, hiding my past like a hand against a photograph.'

8th Air Force veteran, 1987

The old watch tower at Deenethorpe, which was used operationally for 21 months and stood derelict for about 50 years, was sold in 1963 and demolished in the mid 1990s.

There's a "GHOST American airfield" just down the road from Alconbury and it's fast becoming a favourite Yank tourist haunt. The installation – Polebrook, 60 miles north of London – was a beehive of activity during World War – when it served as the HQ of an American outfit. Today, it is as deserted as a haunted house. The haunting atmosphere of the abandoned B-17 base so excites the imagination of some visitors that they swear they are able to detect the roar of Flying Fortresses coming in for a landing – mission completed.'
'Stars and Stripes', 6 October 1958 Deenethorpe

Snetterton Heath airfield, which since the early 1950s has been a motorcycle and racing car circuit and more recently a venue also for Sunday Markets. Top right is the former USAAF repair depot.

Hardwick (Topcroft) airfield's main runway seen through the nose of the BBMF Lancaster.

'The greatest and happiest sound came when we heard the squeal of the landing wheels hitting the runway at home base. We knew then that we had survived. It was interrogation and back to the barracks to fall into our bunks to try to sleep for another dawn.'

Forrest S. Clark, air gunner

'King George VI, his queen and the little princesses visited our base with a lot of brass. We had to fly formation over the field for our visitors for about an hour. We were naturally bitter about this and when they came to our squadron area later, we were still bitching. I was the only one in our barracks who went to the window for a look at them. The King and Queen seemed like very nice people, stopping to chat with passers-by. I doubt that it was their idea for us to fly formation for them. They would have been more considerate…'

Ben Smith

Stearman passing Bury St Edmunds (Rougham) tower.

Flying Eightball at Shipdham in 2007.

Hey paw, tell me again how you and the boys were sweating it out in the E.T.O...'

'English flowers bloom along the runways of the old air base using each and every crack to germinate their yellow, blue and red blossoms. Yet other things take root. There are ghosts that bloom along the runways, silent for years but now stirring in the east-west wind, the same wind that echoes about the ruined control tower. There is a corner of old air base at Shipdham that is particularly haunted. Friends of the Eighth tell of weird sounds and an icy feeling as they pass this corner. The bomber of a green crew rested there in dispersal during 1944. One day returning from a mission the bomber had damage to one engine and made a turn into that side resulting in a spin that sent them down. All died in that crash. But the place where their plane rested is now haunted.

There is a mighty bird that sometimes on fog bound nights, roars along the runway, skimming the concrete cracks and the distant hedgerows.

When I stand on an old abandoned runway or control tower and look out across the old base I hear many sounds. Engines warming up, the roar of take-offs, the squeal of landing wheels as they hit the runway after a long mission and that peculiar squeaking sound and the whisper as the engines were cut off and the bomber came to rest. Above all these sounds there are the faint words of a song that comes back on the slight wind across the English fields like a whisper from our youth, summoning the past. We would be coming back from a mission, tired, disgusted, many times ill from the cold and high-altitude flying. Suddenly, over the intercom, silent on most returns from a mission we would hear a voice singing, "Roll me over, Roll me over, Lay me down and do it again." It's the voice of our navigator, Lieutenant Robert Weatherwax, his flight cap pushed far back on his forehead. However, the most enduring and most vivid ghosts are the friends and fellow crewmembers left behind in the skies. They too haunt the runways and mix like sighs with the wind and the quiet. Who can forget these ghosts of the airfields?"'

Forrest S. Clark

Stearmans airborne at Seething.

Wendling airfield, summer 1994.

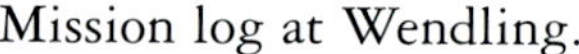

Mission log at Wendling.

'Towards the end of the war Butch, reputedly the oldest American on the base, who worked in the cookhouse, kindly gave me a photograph album. The two covers and the spine of the album were cut and expertly shaped with aluminium from the B-24's bomb bay doors. We then went to several Nissen huts, taking the "pin-ups" off the walls and placing them in my album, a souvenir of those dramatic days. When the Americans went home we spent many weekends and school holidays playing on the deserted base. It was like a ghost town. However, it wasn't long before some of the buildings were in use again. The old briefing building was opened as a village cinema, where we spent many enjoyable evenings watching westerns. After I left school I worked for Corbatch Canners whose factory was at Communal Site #4, which included the former American Red Cross building. In 1945 we moved into the former Officer's Club building, our home for the next eight years. This building still stands and there are murals, which remain to this day."

John Gilbert, who lived on Wendling airfield.

Stearmans over a disused Norfolk airfield in 1994

Broken window panes at Shipdham framing a wartime pin-up.

'It was quite a letdown to see what was offered on the base of the 44th Bomb Group. One of a cluster of airfields in England's East Anglia, our concrete pasture was located near the village of Shipdham, not far from Norwich, in Norfolk County, south of The Wash. The base was an ugly sprawl of Nissen huts and stucco buildings with airplanes to match.'

Keith C. Schuyler, B-24 pilot

A passenger ship at Bovingdon (on a wall now demolished) in 1981.

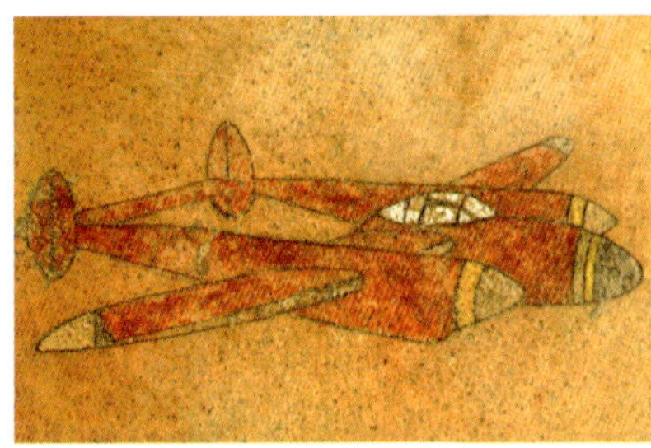

Circus elephant and performer at Flixton in 1991.

'Our jeep driver, a corporal, boasted loudly of how the B-17 had no equal. Ian quietly remarked that we had a twin-engined plane made of wood, called a Mosquito with a crew of two and which carried a heavier bomb load than the B-17. There was an icy silence.'

20-year old Bill Corfield, trainee RAF pilot who landed at Thurleigh

'We had two frustrated Short bomber pilots who thought they should have been made fighter pilots. So, they went to a neighbouring base that had P-38s, checked out, and proceeded to give us one of the best buzz jobs I have ever seen. They came in very low over the cabbage patch next to the Officers' Club, cabbages rolling all over the place, pulled up to go over the club, dropped down again, knocked about 3ft off of the top of a 15ft telephone pole and with parts and pieces trailing, pulled up to about 1,000ft and bailed out. Within minutes, he was at the bar, parachute under one arm and drink in the other. He had to pay for the plane. What a show!'

Colonel Robert H. Tays, pilot, 392nd Bomb Group

Madingley Cemetery the final resting place of more than 3,800 American servicemen. Construction of the cemetery and its memorial was completed in 1956 and the dedication ceremony was held on 16 July 1956. In front of the visitors' building is a 72-ft flagpole and its platform with an inscription on the base taken from John McCrae's poem 'In Flanders Fields'.

'In front of me I saw the field. We banked sharply to the right and we were on the down-wind leg. We let wheels down and turning on the final approach the engineer fired six double red flares – the signal for wounded men on board. "Tower, my brakes are out. My brakes are out," Cowan radioed. As we rolled off the end of the runway to a stop, the ambulance was coming and Chaplain Teska came running. "Chaplain, our radio man, Sparky Sherwyn Meyers," I said.

"What happened?" asked the chaplain.

"20mm in his back." The medic GI's came with stretchers and Sparky was carried out, covered with a blanket, dead. The force of this realization was terrific – I was enraged at Jerry, our enemy and anyone who made us fight. Why did he have to be taken? What was the Lord's plan?

"Sparky had used an ammo box in his radio room to reach his gun and he was up on that box when he was hit.

"He was buried at the Cambridge American Military cemetery, 21 March, Chaplain Teska officiating. Nine crew buddies were there to stand testimony that Sparky will not be forgotten – and there were nine lumps in nine throats as Taps were sounded. The Chaplain said, 'he gave his life that free nations might exist."

"I looked around the cemetery. There were white crosses almost as far as I could see."'

Hank Dibbern, co-pilot, Lieutenant Clement Cowan's crew in the 100th Bomb Group, who later named their Flying Fortress *Sparky*.

'They came from the North, East, South and West - Certain their own state was best...'

'Lieutenant David Edmonds was our original bombardier. He was killed returning from a March 1944 mission to Friedrichshafen when the Scarborough crew crashed in southern England. I never knew what happened to him until many years later at the American Military Cemetery at Madingley. What if I asked if Edmonds was there among the row after row of white crosses? I hesitated to ask because I feared the memories it would stir inside me. Finally I got my nerve up to go into the record office and ask. The clerk took down a giant bound records book and began to look for the name. He ran his finger down the list and lo and behold he found the name. He jotted down the section and plot numbers and handed the slip to me. I declined a military escort and decided to look myself. I walked slowly down among the row after row of crosses fearing what I would find. Finally I stopped. There on a white cross was the name I sought all those years. It hit me like a ton of memories and I was overwhelmed for a moment. I could see his face, hear his laughter, his friendly manner and his love of drinking. I could see him riding to the dispersal area, hear the engines warming up and see him climb aboard. Then, I thought of something else. Edmonds had lost his GI shoes coming overseas and when he went on leave he always wore his bulky flight boots. I said to myself, 'He died with his boots on.' I stood in reverent silence before the white cross but inside I was all in turmoil as memories flooded back. It truly was a religious moment. Finally I turned away by a strong physical effort and walked slowly back amid the sea of white crosses. Thinking still of Edmonds, a few white birds rose into the air before me and I thought at once how futile war had been. How I wished my friend could still be alive and go with me to some village pub and sit and drink a pint of brew and be young again.'

Forrest S. Clark

California graffiti.

Ohio about to be partitioned.

Massachusetts.

Florida and South Carolina.

'Winged Eight' (John Page)

Brambles near wartime barracks at Seething.

Overgrown hut at Flixton.

Ops block at Seething airfield living site.

Winter rain at Flixton.

He may have come from Santa Fe,
He may have known the Great White Way,
Some came who knew Pacific spray
Blowing in from 'Frisco Bay
They came from the North, East, South and West
Certain their own state was best;
Reckless too with love or pay
Then Came to Madingley to stay.
They Came To Madingley **by Jasper Miles**

Most
miss seeing Eddie's ghost!
He sits there oh so still
and probably never will
notice those who pass
his spot in the grass.
Time, for Eddie, ceased in 'forty-four,
he had just two missions more
before returning home Stateside
to take Pauline as his bride;
always showing folks her photograph:
it made his buddies laugh.
After mail-call that day
he was seen to walk away
like he did not want to know
and alone sat down where daisies grow.
Then came the forty-five's loud bang
and men raced to where it rang.
"Shit! Eddie's shot himself! Hell why?"
a friend was heard to cry.
But then he understood better,
picking up and reading Pauline's 'Dear John' letter.'
Eddie's Ghost **by Jasper Miles**

Eerie corridor full of ghosts
at Shipdham in 2007.

BANAN SPETT

The wonderful mural on the wall of the 14th Combat Wing at Shipdham still in remarkable condition in 2007.

There's no fire in the grate now to combat the winter chill at Shipdham.

ACKNOWLEDGEMENTS

Jim Avis, Dave Bagshaw AFC, Carol and Ron Batley, Thorpe Abbotts 100th BG Memorial Museum; Ed Boulter DFC; Mark Brotherton; Walter E. Brown MD, Editor, 8th Air Force Society; John Carter, Tom Chilton, Forrest S. Clark; Bill Corfield; Abel L. Dolim; Bill Espie; Mike Faley; Mike Fuenfer; Gene Gaskins; John Gilbert; Jim Gintner; Larry Goldstein; Steve Gotts; Alan Hague; Clarence 'Buck' G. Haynes; Gerry Honey OBE MRAeS MIMgt; Pete Howard; Peder Larsen; Brian H. Mahoney; Nigel McTeer; Jasper Miles; Bruce Monk; John Page; Richard Page; Wilbur Richardson; Graham M. Simons; Ben Smith Jr.; Milton R. Stokes; Roy West; Paul Wilson.

BIBLIOGRAPHY

Airfield Focus 37: Deenethorpe. John N. Smith. (GMS 1999)
Airfields of The 2nd Air Division, Martin W. Bowman (Pen & Sword 2006)
Airfields of The 1st Air Division, Martin W. Bowman (Pen & Sword 2007)
A Navigator in WWII, William W. Varnedoe Jr.1997 (unpublished)
A Teenage Kansas Farm Boy's Experiences, Dean M. Bloyd
"There we were…or The saga of crew No. 8. Ronald D. Spencer (Manuscript)
452nd BG History.
8th Air Force At War. Memories and Missions, England 1942-45. Martin W. Bowman (PSL 1994)
Century Bombers: The Story of the Bloody Hundredth. Richard Le Strange (100th BG Memorial Museum 1989)
Certified Brave Robert H. Sherwood (unpublished MS)
Chick's Crew: A Tale of the Eighth Air Force. Ben Smith Jr. (Privately Published 1978)
Country Boy-Combat Bomber Pilot Colonel Robert H Tays
Crew Sixty-Four Gene Gaskins. (Privately Published)
Echoes: A Tribute in Verse to the USAAC 1942-45. Jasper Miles
Elusive Horizons, Keith C. Schuyler
Fall Of The Fortresses, The: A personal account of one of the most daring- and deadly – air battles of the Second World War. Elmer Bendiner, Souvenir Press 1980
Fields of Little America. Martin W. Bowman. Wensum Books 1977, PSL & GMS 2003
First of the Many', Captain John R. 'Tex' McCrary and David E. Sherman. (1944)
First Over Germany: A History of the 306th Bomb Group. Russell A. Strong (1982)
Flying School: Combat Hell, Ellis M. Woodward (American Library Press, 1998)
Geoffrey Goreham, *Collective expression of comments, memories, feelings and correspondence of 2nd Air Division veterans during the 1987 Reunion in Norwich.*
In Search of Peace, 453rd BG History. Mike Benarchik.
Letters Home and Other Stuff. Major Ralph H. Elliott (Unpublished)
Light Perpetual: Aviators' Memorial Windows, David Beaty, (Airlife 1995)
Low Level From Swanton, Martin W. Bowman. (ARP 1995)
Might Men of the 381st: Heroes All, The, James Good brown
Skyways to Berlin, Major John M. Redding & Captain Harold Leyshon. Bobbs Merrill, 1943
The Year I Can't Forget, James E. O'Connor
Reluctant Witness. James J. Mahoney and Brian H. Mahoney (Trafford Publishing 2001)
Route As Briefed, The, The history of the 92nd Bombardment Group USAAF 1942-45. John S. Sloan.
Serenade To The Big Bird, Bert Stiles.
467th Bombardment Group, The, Allan Healy (Privately Printed 1947)
Day We Bombed Switzerland, The – Flying with the US 8th AF in WWII, Jackson Granholm (Airlife 2000)
War At My Door, The, Dick Wickham.
Yanks Are Coming, The, Edwin R. W. Hale and John Frayn Turner (Midas Books 1983)
Yesterday's Dragons: The B-17 Flying Fortress over Europe during WWII. Abel L. Dolim (2001)